50 Barbecue Delicious Recipes

By: Kelly Johnson

Table of Contents

- Pulled Pork Sandwiches
- Baby Back Ribs
- Grilled Chicken Wings
- BBQ Brisket
- Grilled Sausages
- BBQ Chicken Thighs
- Grilled Shrimp Skewers
- Smoked Sausages
- BBQ Pork Ribs
- Grilled Corn on the Cob
- Barbecue Meatballs
- Grilled Steak
- Burnt Ends
- Grilled Lamb Chops
- BBQ Beef Sliders
- Grilled Veggie Skewers
- Smoked Turkey Legs

- BBQ Pulled Jackfruit
- Grilled Pineapple
- Barbecue Chicken Drumsticks
- Grilled Fish Tacos
- BBQ Beef Brisket Sandwiches
- Grilled Asparagus
- BBQ Baked Beans
- Grilled Portobello Mushrooms
- Smoked Ribs
- BBQ Chicken Legs
- Grilled Eggplant
- BBQ Pulled Chicken
- Grilled Bell Peppers
- Grilled Sweet Potatoes
- Barbecue Pork Belly
- Grilled Flatbreads
- Smoked Lamb Shoulder
- BBQ Sliders with Coleslaw
- Grilled Shrimp and Grits

- Grilled Tomatoes
- BBQ Beef Tenderloin
- Grilled Salmon
- BBQ Stuffed Peppers
- Grilled Zucchini
- BBQ Chicken Breast
- Grilled Bacon-Wrapped Asparagus
- Smoked Fish Fillets
- BBQ Sausage and Peppers
- Grilled Broccoli with Lemon
- Barbecue Meatloaf
- Grilled Tofu Skewers
- BBQ Cornbread
- Grilled Onion Rings

Pulled Pork Sandwiches

Ingredients:

- 2 lbs pork shoulder or butt
- 1 cup BBQ sauce
- 1 onion, sliced
- 1 cup chicken broth
- 1 tbsp paprika
- 1 tbsp brown sugar
- 1 tsp garlic powder
- 1 tsp onion powder
- Salt and pepper to taste
- 4 hamburger buns
- Coleslaw (optional, for topping)

Instructions:

1. Preheat the oven to 300°F (150°C).
2. Rub the pork with paprika, brown sugar, garlic powder, onion powder, salt, and pepper.
3. Place the pork in a large Dutch oven with the sliced onion and chicken broth.
4. Cover and cook in the oven for 3-4 hours until the pork is tender and easily pulled apart.

5. Remove the pork from the oven and shred with two forks.

6. Mix the shredded pork with BBQ sauce.

7. Serve on hamburger buns, topped with coleslaw if desired.

Baby Back Ribs

Ingredients:

- 2 racks of baby back ribs
- 1/4 cup brown sugar
- 2 tbsp paprika
- 1 tbsp garlic powder
- 1 tbsp onion powder
- 1 tbsp chili powder
- Salt and pepper to taste
- 1 cup BBQ sauce

Instructions:

1. Preheat the grill to medium heat or preheat the oven to 300°F (150°C).
2. Mix brown sugar, paprika, garlic powder, onion powder, chili powder, salt, and pepper in a bowl.
3. Rub the ribs with the seasoning mixture on both sides.
4. If grilling: Place the ribs on the grill and cook for 2-3 hours, turning occasionally and basting with BBQ sauce.
5. If baking: Wrap the ribs in foil and bake for 2-3 hours in the oven. Unwrap and brush with BBQ sauce, then bake for an additional 30 minutes.
6. Serve hot with extra BBQ sauce.

Grilled Chicken Wings

Ingredients:

- 12 chicken wings
- 2 tbsp olive oil
- 1 tbsp soy sauce
- 1 tbsp honey
- 1 tsp garlic powder
- 1 tsp paprika
- Salt and pepper to taste
- BBQ sauce (optional)

Instructions:

1. Preheat the grill to medium heat.
2. In a bowl, mix olive oil, soy sauce, honey, garlic powder, paprika, salt, and pepper.
3. Toss the chicken wings in the marinade and let sit for at least 30 minutes.
4. Grill the wings for 20-25 minutes, turning occasionally, until crispy and cooked through.
5. Brush with BBQ sauce if desired and serve hot.

BBQ Brisket

Ingredients:

- 4 lbs beef brisket
- 1/4 cup brown sugar
- 2 tbsp paprika
- 1 tbsp garlic powder
- 1 tbsp onion powder
- 1 tbsp chili powder
- 2 tsp black pepper
- 1 tsp salt
- 1 cup beef broth
- 1 cup BBQ sauce

Instructions:

1. Preheat the oven to 300°F (150°C).
2. Mix brown sugar, paprika, garlic powder, onion powder, chili powder, black pepper, and salt in a bowl.
3. Rub the brisket with the seasoning mixture.
4. Place the brisket in a roasting pan and add beef broth.
5. Cover with foil and roast for 3-4 hours until tender.
6. Remove the foil, brush with BBQ sauce, and cook for an additional 30 minutes.

7. Slice and serve with extra BBQ sauce.

Grilled Sausages

Ingredients:

- 8 sausages (your choice of flavor)
- 1 tbsp olive oil
- Salt and pepper

Instructions:

1. Preheat the grill to medium heat.
2. Brush the sausages with olive oil and season with salt and pepper.
3. Grill the sausages for 12-15 minutes, turning occasionally, until they are browned and cooked through.
4. Serve with your favorite condiments.

BBQ Chicken Thighs

Ingredients:

- 6 chicken thighs (bone-in, skin-on)
- 1/4 cup BBQ sauce
- Salt and pepper to taste

Instructions:

1. Preheat the grill to medium heat.
2. Season the chicken thighs with salt and pepper.
3. Grill the chicken for 5-7 minutes per side, brushing with BBQ sauce during the last few minutes of grilling.
4. Cook until the internal temperature reaches 165°F (75°C).
5. Serve with extra BBQ sauce.

Grilled Shrimp Skewers

Ingredients:

- 1 lb shrimp, peeled and deveined
- 2 tbsp olive oil
- 1 tbsp lemon juice
- 2 garlic cloves, minced
- 1 tsp paprika
- Salt and pepper to taste
- Skewers (if wooden, soak in water for 30 minutes)

Instructions:

1. Preheat the grill to medium-high heat.
2. In a bowl, mix olive oil, lemon juice, garlic, paprika, salt, and pepper.
3. Toss the shrimp in the marinade and let sit for 15 minutes.
4. Thread the shrimp onto skewers.
5. Grill the shrimp for 2-3 minutes per side until pink and opaque.
6. Serve with lemon wedges.

Smoked Sausages

Ingredients:

- 4 sausages (your choice of flavor)
- Wood chips for smoking

Instructions:

1. Preheat the smoker to 225°F (107°C).
2. Add wood chips to the smoker according to manufacturer instructions.
3. Place the sausages in the smoker and cook for 1-1.5 hours, turning occasionally.
4. Serve hot with your favorite condiments.

Grilled Shrimp Skewers

Ingredients:

- 1 lb shrimp, peeled and deveined
- 2 tbsp olive oil
- 1 tbsp lemon juice
- 2 garlic cloves, minced
- 1 tsp paprika
- Salt and pepper to taste
- Skewers (if wooden, soak in water for 30 minutes)

Instructions:

1. Preheat the grill to medium-high heat.
2. In a bowl, mix olive oil, lemon juice, garlic, paprika, salt, and pepper.
3. Toss the shrimp in the marinade and let sit for 15 minutes.
4. Thread the shrimp onto skewers.
5. Grill the shrimp for 2-3 minutes per side until pink and opaque.
6. Serve with lemon wedges.

Smoked Sausages

Ingredients:

- 4 sausages (your choice of flavor)
- Wood chips for smoking

Instructions:

1. Preheat the smoker to 225°F (107°C).
2. Add wood chips to the smoker according to manufacturer instructions.
3. Place the sausages in the smoker and cook for 1-1.5 hours, turning occasionally.
4. Serve hot with your favorite condiments.

BBQ Pork Ribs

Ingredients:

- 2 racks of pork ribs
- 1/4 cup brown sugar
- 2 tbsp paprika
- 1 tbsp garlic powder
- 1 tbsp onion powder
- 1 tbsp chili powder
- Salt and pepper to taste
- 1 cup BBQ sauce

Instructions:

1. Preheat the grill to medium heat or preheat the oven to 300°F (150°C).
2. Mix brown sugar, paprika, garlic powder, onion powder, chili powder, salt, and pepper in a bowl.
3. Rub the ribs with the seasoning mixture on both sides.
4. If grilling: Place the ribs on the grill and cook for 2-3 hours, turning occasionally and basting with BBQ sauce.
5. If baking: Wrap the ribs in foil and bake for 2-3 hours in the oven. Unwrap and brush with BBQ sauce, then bake for an additional 30 minutes.
6. Serve hot with extra BBQ sauce.

Grilled Corn on the Cob

Ingredients:

- 4 ears of corn, husked
- 2 tbsp olive oil or butter
- Salt and pepper to taste
- Lime wedges (optional)

Instructions:

1. Preheat the grill to medium-high heat.
2. Brush the corn with olive oil or butter and season with salt and pepper.
3. Grill the corn for 10-15 minutes, turning occasionally, until it's charred and tender.
4. Serve with lime wedges and additional butter if desired.

Barbecue Meatballs

Ingredients:

- 1 lb ground beef or pork
- 1/4 cup breadcrumbs
- 1/4 cup grated Parmesan
- 1 egg
- 2 garlic cloves, minced
- 1 tbsp Italian seasoning
- 1/2 cup BBQ sauce

Instructions:

1. Preheat the oven to 375°F (190°C).
2. In a bowl, combine the ground meat, breadcrumbs, Parmesan, egg, garlic, and Italian seasoning.
3. Form the mixture into 1-inch meatballs and place them on a baking sheet.
4. Bake for 15-20 minutes until cooked through.
5. Brush with BBQ sauce and bake for an additional 5 minutes.
6. Serve hot with extra BBQ sauce on the side.

Grilled Steak

Ingredients:

- 2 steaks (ribeye, sirloin, or your choice)
- 2 tbsp olive oil
- 1 tbsp garlic powder
- 1 tbsp onion powder
- Salt and pepper to taste

Instructions:

1. Preheat the grill to high heat.
2. Rub the steaks with olive oil, garlic powder, onion powder, salt, and pepper.
3. Grill the steaks for 4-6 minutes per side for medium-rare, or adjust to your desired doneness.
4. Let the steaks rest for 5 minutes before serving.

Burnt Ends

Ingredients:

- 3 lbs beef brisket, cut into cubes
- 1/4 cup BBQ rub (store-bought or homemade)
- 1/2 cup BBQ sauce
- 2 tbsp honey
- 2 tbsp butter

Instructions:

1. Preheat the smoker to 225°F (107°C).
2. Coat the brisket cubes with BBQ rub.
3. Smoke the beef cubes for 2-3 hours, until they reach an internal temperature of 195°F (90°C).
4. Mix BBQ sauce, honey, and butter, and toss the cooked cubes in the sauce.
5. Return the cubes to the smoker for another hour until caramelized.
6. Serve hot.

Grilled Lamb Chops

Ingredients:

- 8 lamb chops
- 2 tbsp olive oil
- 2 garlic cloves, minced
- 1 tbsp fresh rosemary, chopped
- Salt and pepper to taste

Instructions:

1. Preheat the grill to medium-high heat.
2. Brush the lamb chops with olive oil and season with garlic, rosemary, salt, and pepper.
3. Grill the lamb chops for 3-4 minutes per side for medium-rare.
4. Let them rest for 5 minutes before serving.

BBQ Beef Sliders

Ingredients:

- 1 lb ground beef
- 1/2 cup BBQ sauce
- 1 tbsp Worcestershire sauce
- 12 slider buns
- Cheese slices (optional)
- Pickles and onions for topping

Instructions:

1. Preheat the grill to medium-high heat.
2. Form the ground beef into small slider patties and season with salt and pepper.
3. Grill the sliders for 3-4 minutes per side, adding cheese during the last minute of cooking if desired.
4. Brush with BBQ sauce and serve on slider buns with pickles and onions.

Grilled Veggie Skewers

Ingredients:

- 1 zucchini, sliced
- 1 bell pepper, cut into chunks
- 1 red onion, cut into chunks
- 8 oz mushrooms, whole or halved
- 1 tbsp olive oil
- Salt and pepper to taste

Instructions:

1. Preheat the grill to medium-high heat.
2. Thread the vegetables onto skewers, alternating as you go.
3. Brush the veggies with olive oil and season with salt and pepper.
4. Grill the skewers for 8-10 minutes, turning occasionally, until the vegetables are tender and lightly charred.
5. Serve hot.

Smoked Turkey Legs

Ingredients:

- 4 turkey legs
- 1/4 cup olive oil
- 2 tbsp paprika
- 1 tbsp garlic powder
- 1 tbsp onion powder
- Salt and pepper to taste
- Wood chips for smoking

Instructions:

1. Preheat the smoker to 225°F (107°C).
2. Rub the turkey legs with olive oil, paprika, garlic powder, onion powder, salt, and pepper.
3. Place the turkey legs in the smoker and smoke for 2-3 hours, or until the internal temperature reaches 165°F (75°C).
4. Serve with your favorite dipping sauce.

BBQ Pulled Jackfruit

Ingredients:

- 2 cans young green jackfruit in brine, drained and shredded
- 1 cup BBQ sauce
- 1 tbsp olive oil
- 1/2 onion, chopped
- 2 garlic cloves, minced
- Salt and pepper to taste

Instructions:

1. In a large pan, heat olive oil over medium heat and sauté onion and garlic until softened.
2. Add the shredded jackfruit and cook for 5-7 minutes, stirring occasionally.
3. Pour in the BBQ sauce and simmer for 10-15 minutes, until heated through and tender.
4. Serve on buns with coleslaw for a vegetarian BBQ option.

Grilled Pineapple

Ingredients:

- 1 pineapple, peeled and sliced into rings
- 2 tbsp honey
- 1 tbsp lime juice
- 1/2 tsp cinnamon (optional)

Instructions:

1. Preheat the grill to medium heat.
2. Brush the pineapple rings with honey and lime juice.
3. Grill the pineapple for 3-4 minutes per side, until caramelized and grill marks appear.
4. Sprinkle with cinnamon if desired and serve hot.

Barbecue Chicken Drumsticks

Ingredients:

- 10 chicken drumsticks
- 1/4 cup olive oil
- 1/4 cup BBQ sauce
- 1 tbsp paprika
- 1 tbsp garlic powder
- Salt and pepper to taste

Instructions:

1. Preheat the grill to medium heat.
2. Rub the chicken drumsticks with olive oil, paprika, garlic powder, salt, and pepper.
3. Grill the drumsticks for 25-30 minutes, turning every 5-7 minutes, until the internal temperature reaches 165°F (74°C).
4. Brush the chicken with BBQ sauce during the last 5 minutes of grilling.
5. Serve hot.

Grilled Fish Tacos

Ingredients:

- 4 white fish fillets (like tilapia or cod)
- 1 tbsp olive oil
- 1 tsp chili powder
- 1 tsp cumin
- Salt and pepper to taste
- 8 small corn tortillas
- Cabbage slaw (for topping)
- Lime wedges (for garnish)

Instructions:

1. Preheat the grill to medium-high heat.
2. Drizzle the fish fillets with olive oil and season with chili powder, cumin, salt, and pepper.
3. Grill the fish for 4-5 minutes per side, or until the fish flakes easily with a fork.
4. Warm the tortillas on the grill for 1 minute per side.
5. Flake the grilled fish and serve in the tortillas with cabbage slaw and lime wedges.

BBQ Beef Brisket Sandwiches

Ingredients:

- 3 lb beef brisket
- 1/4 cup BBQ rub (store-bought or homemade)
- 1 cup BBQ sauce
- 6 sandwich buns
- Pickles (optional)

Instructions:

1. Preheat the smoker to 225°F (107°C).
2. Rub the brisket with BBQ rub and place it in the smoker.
3. Smoke the brisket for 6-8 hours, or until the internal temperature reaches 195°F (90°C).
4. Slice the brisket and toss with BBQ sauce.
5. Serve the brisket on sandwich buns with pickles.

Grilled Asparagus

Ingredients:

- 1 lb asparagus, trimmed
- 1 tbsp olive oil
- Salt and pepper to taste
- 1 tbsp lemon juice (optional)

Instructions:

1. Preheat the grill to medium heat.
2. Toss the asparagus with olive oil, salt, and pepper.
3. Grill the asparagus for 5-7 minutes, turning occasionally, until tender and lightly charred.
4. Drizzle with lemon juice before serving (optional).

BBQ Baked Beans

Ingredients:

- 2 cans baked beans (or 4 cups homemade beans)
- 1/2 cup BBQ sauce
- 1/2 onion, diced
- 1/2 cup bacon, cooked and crumbled (optional)

Instructions:

1. Preheat the oven to 350°F (175°C).
2. In a baking dish, combine the baked beans, BBQ sauce, onion, and bacon.
3. Bake for 30-40 minutes, stirring occasionally, until bubbly and thickened.
4. Serve as a side dish with your BBQ.

Grilled Portobello Mushrooms

Ingredients:

- 4 large portobello mushrooms
- 2 tbsp olive oil
- 1 tbsp balsamic vinegar
- 1 garlic clove, minced
- Salt and pepper to taste

Instructions:

1. Preheat the grill to medium-high heat.
2. Clean the mushrooms and remove the stems.
3. Drizzle with olive oil, balsamic vinegar, garlic, salt, and pepper.
4. Grill the mushrooms for 5-7 minutes per side, until tender.
5. Serve as a side or on a burger bun.

Smoked Ribs

Ingredients:

- 2 racks baby back ribs
- 1/4 cup BBQ rub
- 1 cup BBQ sauce

Instructions:

1. Preheat the smoker to 225°F (107°C).
2. Remove the membrane from the ribs and apply BBQ rub on both sides.
3. Smoke the ribs for 4-6 hours, or until they are tender and the internal temperature reaches 190°F (88°C).
4. Brush the ribs with BBQ sauce during the last 30 minutes of smoking.
5. Let rest for 10 minutes, then slice and serve.

BBQ Chicken Legs

Ingredients:

- 8 chicken legs
- 1/4 cup olive oil
- 1/4 cup BBQ sauce
- Salt and pepper to taste

Instructions:

1. Preheat the grill to medium-high heat.
2. Coat the chicken legs with olive oil, salt, pepper, and BBQ sauce.
3. Grill the chicken legs for 25-30 minutes, turning every 7 minutes, until the internal temperature reaches 165°F (74°C).
4. Serve with extra BBQ sauce.

Grilled Eggplant

Ingredients:

- 2 eggplants, sliced into 1-inch rounds
- 2 tbsp olive oil
- Salt and pepper to taste
- 1 tbsp balsamic vinegar (optional)

Instructions:

1. Preheat the grill to medium heat.
2. Brush the eggplant slices with olive oil, salt, and pepper.
3. Grill the eggplant for 3-4 minutes per side, until tender and grill marks appear.
4. Drizzle with balsamic vinegar if desired and serve.

BBQ Pulled Chicken

Ingredients:

- 4 chicken breasts or thighs
- 1/2 cup BBQ sauce
- 1/2 cup chicken broth
- 1 tbsp olive oil
- 6 sandwich buns

Instructions:

1. Heat olive oil in a large pan over medium heat.
2. Add chicken breasts or thighs and cook until browned on both sides, about 5-7 minutes.
3. Add chicken broth and BBQ sauce, then cover and simmer for 25-30 minutes, or until the chicken is cooked through.
4. Shred the chicken with two forks and toss in the sauce.
5. Serve the pulled chicken on sandwich buns.

Grilled Bell Peppers

Ingredients:

- 4 bell peppers (any color)
- 2 tbsp olive oil
- Salt and pepper to taste
- 1 tsp dried oregano (optional)

Instructions:

1. Preheat the grill to medium-high heat.
2. Cut the bell peppers in half and remove the seeds and membranes.
3. Drizzle the peppers with olive oil and season with salt, pepper, and oregano.
4. Grill the peppers, cut-side down, for 5-7 minutes, until tender and charred.
5. Serve as a side or in salads, sandwiches, or wraps.

Grilled Sweet Potatoes

Ingredients:

- 4 sweet potatoes
- 2 tbsp olive oil
- Salt and pepper to taste
- 1 tsp cinnamon (optional)

Instructions:

1. Preheat the grill to medium heat.
2. Slice the sweet potatoes into 1/2-inch thick rounds.
3. Drizzle with olive oil and season with salt, pepper, and cinnamon (if using).
4. Grill the slices for 5-7 minutes per side, until tender and lightly charred.
5. Serve as a side dish.

Barbecue Pork Belly

Ingredients:

- 2 lb pork belly, skin-on
- 1/4 cup BBQ rub
- 1/2 cup BBQ sauce

Instructions:

1. Preheat the smoker or grill to 250°F (121°C).
2. Rub the pork belly with BBQ rub.
3. Smoke for 4-5 hours, until the internal temperature reaches 190°F (88°C).
4. During the last 30 minutes, brush the pork belly with BBQ sauce.
5. Let rest for 10 minutes before slicing and serving.

Grilled Flatbreads

Ingredients:

- 2 cups all-purpose flour
- 1 tsp yeast
- 1/2 tsp salt
- 1/2 cup warm water
- 2 tbsp olive oil

Instructions:

1. Mix the yeast and warm water in a bowl and let sit for 5 minutes.
2. Combine flour, salt, and olive oil in a mixing bowl. Gradually add the yeast mixture and knead to form a dough.
3. Let the dough rise for 1 hour.
4. Preheat the grill to medium-high heat.
5. Divide the dough into small balls, roll each into a flat round, and grill for 2-3 minutes per side, until golden and puffed.
6. Serve with dips or as a base for toppings.

Smoked Lamb Shoulder

Ingredients:

- 4 lb lamb shoulder
- 2 tbsp olive oil
- 2 tbsp garlic powder
- 1 tbsp rosemary
- Salt and pepper to taste
- 1 cup broth (for smoking)

Instructions:

1. Preheat the smoker to 225°F (107°C).
2. Rub the lamb shoulder with olive oil, garlic powder, rosemary, salt, and pepper.
3. Smoke the lamb for 4-5 hours, until the internal temperature reaches 195°F (90°C).
4. Let the lamb rest for 15 minutes before slicing.
5. Serve with your favorite sides.

BBQ Sliders with Coleslaw

Ingredients:

- 1 lb ground beef or pork
- 1 tbsp BBQ sauce
- 1/2 tsp salt
- 1/4 tsp pepper
- 12 slider buns
- 1 cup coleslaw mix
- 1/4 cup coleslaw dressing

Instructions:

1. Preheat the grill to medium-high heat.
2. Mix the ground meat with BBQ sauce, salt, and pepper.
3. Form into small patties and grill for 3-4 minutes per side, until cooked through.
4. Mix the coleslaw mix with coleslaw dressing.
5. Assemble the sliders by placing the patties on the buns and topping with coleslaw.
6. Serve immediately.

Grilled Shrimp and Grits

Ingredients:

- 1 lb shrimp, peeled and deveined
- 1 tbsp olive oil
- 1 tsp paprika
- 1/2 tsp garlic powder
- 1 cup grits
- 4 cups water
- 1/2 cup heavy cream
- Salt and pepper to taste

Instructions:

1. Preheat the grill to medium-high heat.
2. Toss the shrimp with olive oil, paprika, garlic powder, salt, and pepper.
3. Grill the shrimp for 2-3 minutes per side, until pink and cooked through.
4. Cook the grits according to package instructions, adding heavy cream to make them creamy.
5. Serve the shrimp on top of the grits.

Grilled Tomatoes

Ingredients:

- 6 medium tomatoes
- 2 tbsp olive oil
- Salt and pepper to taste
- Fresh basil leaves (optional)

Instructions:

1. Preheat the grill to medium heat.
2. Cut the tomatoes in half and remove the seeds.
3. Drizzle with olive oil and season with salt and pepper.
4. Grill the tomatoes, cut-side down, for 4-5 minutes, until lightly charred.
5. Garnish with fresh basil if desired and serve as a side or in salads.

BBQ Beef Tenderloin

Ingredients:

- 2 lb beef tenderloin
- 2 tbsp olive oil
- 1 tbsp garlic powder
- 1 tbsp rosemary
- Salt and pepper to taste
- 1/4 cup BBQ sauce

Instructions:

1. Preheat the grill to medium-high heat.
2. Rub the beef tenderloin with olive oil, garlic powder, rosemary, salt, and pepper.
3. Grill the tenderloin for 20-25 minutes, turning every 5 minutes, until the internal temperature reaches 130°F (54°C) for medium-rare.
4. Brush with BBQ sauce during the last 5 minutes of grilling.
5. Let the beef rest for 10 minutes before slicing and serving.

Grilled Salmon

Ingredients:

- 4 salmon fillets
- 2 tbsp olive oil
- Salt and pepper to taste
- 1 tbsp lemon juice
- Fresh herbs (like dill or parsley) for garnish

Instructions:

1. Preheat the grill to medium-high heat.
2. Brush the salmon fillets with olive oil and season with salt and pepper.
3. Place the salmon on the grill, skin-side down, and cook for 4-5 minutes per side, until the fish flakes easily with a fork.
4. Drizzle with lemon juice and garnish with fresh herbs before serving.

BBQ Stuffed Peppers

Ingredients:

- 4 bell peppers
- 1 lb ground beef or turkey
- 1 cup cooked rice
- 1 cup BBQ sauce
- 1/2 cup shredded cheese
- Salt and pepper to taste

Instructions:

1. Preheat the grill to medium heat.
2. Slice the tops off the bell peppers and remove the seeds.
3. In a skillet, cook the ground meat, then mix with cooked rice, BBQ sauce, salt, and pepper.
4. Stuff the peppers with the meat and rice mixture and top with shredded cheese.
5. Grill the stuffed peppers for 10-15 minutes, until the peppers are tender and the cheese is melted.

Grilled Zucchini

Ingredients:

- 4 zucchinis, sliced lengthwise
- 2 tbsp olive oil
- Salt and pepper to taste
- 1 tsp garlic powder (optional)
- Fresh basil or parsley for garnish

Instructions:

1. Preheat the grill to medium-high heat.
2. Brush the zucchini slices with olive oil and season with salt, pepper, and garlic powder.
3. Grill the zucchini for 3-4 minutes per side, until lightly charred and tender.
4. Garnish with fresh basil or parsley before serving.

BBQ Chicken Breast

Ingredients:

- 4 chicken breasts
- 1/4 cup BBQ sauce
- Salt and pepper to taste

Instructions:

1. Preheat the grill to medium heat.
2. Season the chicken breasts with salt and pepper.
3. Grill the chicken for 5-6 minutes per side, until the internal temperature reaches 165°F (74°C).
4. During the last 2 minutes of grilling, brush with BBQ sauce.
5. Let the chicken rest for a few minutes before serving.

Grilled Bacon-Wrapped Asparagus

Ingredients:

- 1 bunch asparagus
- 8 slices of bacon
- Salt and pepper to taste

Instructions:

1. Preheat the grill to medium-high heat.
2. Trim the tough ends of the asparagus and season with salt and pepper.
3. Wrap 4-5 spears of asparagus with one slice of bacon.
4. Grill the bacon-wrapped asparagus for 4-5 minutes per side, until the bacon is crispy and the asparagus is tender.

Smoked Fish Fillets

Ingredients:

- 4 fish fillets (like trout or white fish)
- 2 tbsp olive oil
- 1 tbsp lemon juice
- Salt and pepper to taste
- Wood chips for smoking

Instructions:

1. Preheat the smoker to 225°F (107°C).
2. Drizzle the fish fillets with olive oil and lemon juice, and season with salt and pepper.
3. Place the fillets in the smoker and cook for 1-2 hours, depending on the thickness of the fillets, until the fish is flaky and fully cooked.
4. Serve with fresh herbs or lemon wedges.

BBQ Sausage and Peppers

Ingredients:

- 4 sausages (your choice of type)
- 2 bell peppers, sliced
- 1 onion, sliced
- 1 tbsp olive oil
- Salt and pepper to taste

Instructions:

1. Preheat the grill to medium heat.
2. Grill the sausages for 6-8 minutes per side, until cooked through.
3. Meanwhile, toss the peppers and onions with olive oil, salt, and pepper.
4. Grill the peppers and onions for 6-8 minutes, until tender and slightly charred.
5. Serve the sausages with the grilled peppers and onions.

Grilled Broccoli with Lemon

Ingredients:

- 1 bunch broccoli, cut into florets
- 2 tbsp olive oil
- 1 tbsp lemon juice
- Salt and pepper to taste
- Lemon zest for garnish

Instructions:

1. Preheat the grill to medium heat.
2. Toss the broccoli florets with olive oil, salt, and pepper.
3. Grill the broccoli for 4-5 minutes, until charred and tender.
4. Drizzle with lemon juice and garnish with lemon zest before serving.

Barbecue Meatloaf

Ingredients:

- 1 lb ground beef or pork
- 1/2 cup breadcrumbs
- 1 egg
- 1/4 cup BBQ sauce, plus extra for glazing
- 1/2 onion, finely chopped
- 1 tsp garlic powder
- Salt and pepper to taste

Instructions:

1. Preheat the grill to medium heat.
2. In a large bowl, combine the ground meat, breadcrumbs, egg, BBQ sauce, onion, garlic powder, salt, and pepper.
3. Form the mixture into a loaf shape and place it on the grill.
4. Grill the meatloaf for 25-30 minutes, until fully cooked, glazing with extra BBQ sauce during the last 5 minutes.
5. Let the meatloaf rest for 10 minutes before slicing and serving.

Grilled Tofu Skewers

Ingredients:

- 1 block firm tofu, drained and pressed
- 2 tbsp olive oil
- 2 tbsp soy sauce
- 1 tbsp maple syrup or honey
- 1 tsp garlic powder
- 1 tsp smoked paprika
- Salt and pepper to taste
- Wooden skewers (soaked in water for 30 minutes)

Instructions:

1. Preheat the grill to medium heat.
2. Cut the pressed tofu into cubes and place in a bowl.
3. In a separate bowl, mix together olive oil, soy sauce, maple syrup, garlic powder, smoked paprika, salt, and pepper.
4. Toss the tofu cubes in the marinade and let it sit for at least 10-15 minutes.
5. Thread the marinated tofu onto the skewers.
6. Grill the tofu skewers for 4-5 minutes per side, turning occasionally, until golden and slightly crispy on the outside.
7. Serve with a dipping sauce like peanut or sriracha mayo if desired.

BBQ Cornbread

Ingredients:

- 1 cup cornmeal
- 1 cup all-purpose flour
- 1/4 cup sugar
- 1 tbsp baking powder
- 1/2 tsp salt
- 1 cup milk
- 2 eggs
- 1/4 cup melted butter
- 1/2 cup BBQ sauce (plus more for drizzling)
- 1/2 cup corn kernels (optional)
- 1/2 cup shredded cheddar cheese (optional)

Instructions:

1. Preheat the grill to medium heat.
2. In a large bowl, combine cornmeal, flour, sugar, baking powder, and salt.
3. In a separate bowl, whisk together milk, eggs, melted butter, and BBQ sauce.
4. Add the wet ingredients to the dry ingredients and mix until just combined.
5. If using, fold in corn kernels and shredded cheddar cheese.
6. Pour the batter into a greased 9x9-inch baking pan or cast-iron skillet.
7. Place the pan on the grill and cook with the lid closed for 20-30 minutes, until a toothpick inserted into the center comes out clean.

8. Drizzle with extra BBQ sauce before serving.

Grilled Onion Rings

Ingredients:

- 2 large onions, sliced into rings
- 1 cup flour
- 1 tsp garlic powder
- 1 tsp smoked paprika
- Salt and pepper to taste
- 1 cup buttermilk
- 1/2 cup breadcrumbs
- Olive oil for brushing

Instructions:

1. Preheat the grill to medium heat.
2. In a bowl, combine flour, garlic powder, smoked paprika, salt, and pepper.
3. In a separate bowl, place the buttermilk.
4. Dredge the onion rings first in the flour mixture, then dip in the buttermilk, and finally coat with breadcrumbs.
5. Brush the onion rings lightly with olive oil to prevent sticking.
6. Place the onion rings on the grill and cook for 3-4 minutes per side, until crispy and golden.
7. Serve with dipping sauce like ranch or BBQ sauce.